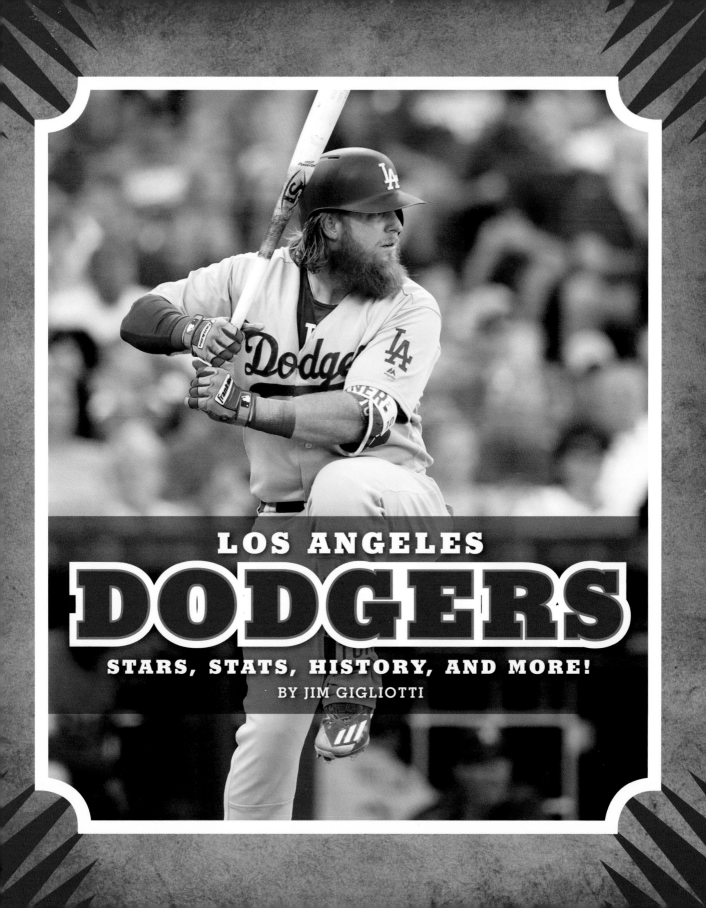

LOS ANGELES
DODGERS
STARS, STATS, HISTORY, AND MORE!
BY JIM GIGLIOTTI

Published by The Child's World®
1980 Lookout Drive • Mankato, MN 56003-1705
800-599-READ • www.childsworld.com

ISBN 9781503828278
LCCN 2018944840

Printed in the United States of America
PAO2392

Photo Credits:
Cover: Joe Robbins (2).
Inside: Alamy Stock: PicturesNow 9; AP Images: 17, 23,
David Durochik 29; Dreamstime.com: Ffooter 14, 20;
Library of Congress: 5; Newscom: Lori Shepler/UPI 6, 19;
Joe Robbins: 10, 24, 27; Shutterstock: Kit Leong 12.

About the Author

Jim Gigliotti has worked for
the University of Southern
California's athletic
department, the Los Angeles
Dodgers, and the National
Football League. He is now an
author who has written more
than 80 books, mostly for
young readers, on a variety
of topics.

On the Cover

Main photo: Third baseman
Justin Turner
Inset: Hall of Fame pitcher
Sandy Koufax

CONTENTS

GO, DODGERS!

The Dodgers are very important to baseball history. They are one of the best teams ever. Only a handful of teams have won more titles. They've done big things off the field, too. The Dodgers were the first modern team to **sign** an African American player. They also helped make baseball a truly national game. Let's find out how. Let's meet the Dodgers!

In 1947, Jackie Robinson became MLB's first ➤
African American player in the 20th century.

WHO ARE THE DODGERS?

The Dodgers play in the National League (NL). That group is part of Major League Baseball (MLB). MLB also includes the American League (AL). There are 30 teams in MLB. The winner of the NL plays the winner of the AL in the **World Series**. The Dodgers have played in the World Series 20 times. They have won the championship six times.

◄ *Joc Pederson celebrated after hitting a homer in the 2017 World Series.*

WHERE THEY CAME FROM

The Dodgers started in Brooklyn, New York, in 1884. The team has had many names. They have been called Dodgers since 1932. That name was used because their fans had to **dodge** trolley cars in Brooklyn! In 1958, the Dodgers moved to Los Angeles. The Dodgers and the San Francisco Giants became the first big-league teams in California.

The Brooklyn Dodgers played at Ebbets Field. ➤
Brooklyn is a borough, or part, of New York City.

WHO THEY PLAY

The Dodgers play 162 games each season. There are 81 home games and 81 road games. Most of their games are against other NL teams. Their fans always get up for the games against the Giants. The Dodgers and Giants don't like each other very much! The **rivals** have faced off for more than 100 years. They first played each other in 1890!

◄ *Chris Taylor tracks a fly ball for the Dodgers against the Giants.*

WHERE THEY PLAY

The Dodgers play at Dodger Stadium. It opened in 1962. It is one of the oldest parks in MLB. Fenway Park in Boston is the oldest. Wrigley Field in Chicago is next. But Dodger Stadium is still one of the most beautiful places to watch a game. It gets a fresh coat of "Dodger Blue" paint every year. The stadium has great views of Los Angeles.

Fireworks often burst above Dodger Stadium after summer ballgames. ➤

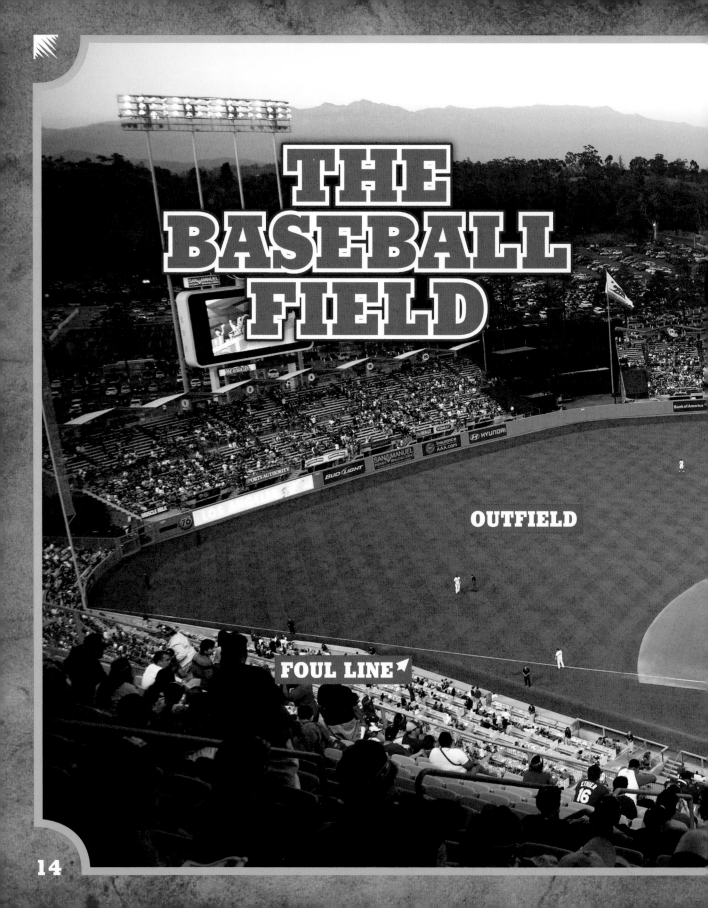

THE BASEBALL FIELD

OUTFIELD

FOUL LINE ➔

FOUL LINE ➤

▼ SECOND BASE

INFIELD

▼ FIRST BASE

▲ DUGOUT

▼ THIRD BASE

▲ PITCHER'S MOUND

ON-DECK CIRCLE ◄

▲ COACH'S BOX

▲ HOME PLATE

BIG DAYS

In 1988, LA's Kirk Gibson hit a famous home run. It beat the Oakland A's in a World Series game. The Dodgers have had lots of other big days, too.

1955—The Dodgers had many good teams in the 1950s. They often came close, but didn't win a title. "Wait 'til next year!" their fans said. In 1955, next year came. The Dodgers beat the New York Yankees 2–0 in Game 7 of the World Series.

1965—Sandy Koufax tossed a perfect game against the Cubs. That means 27 batters up and 27 down. It's one of the hardest things to do in baseball. Koufax struck out 14 in the game. The Dodgers won 1–0.

Sandy Koufax's perfect game was the fourth no-hitter of his great career. ➤

2004—The Dodgers beat the Giants 7–3 to win the NL West division. It wasn't just that they won. It was how they won. The Dodgers trailed 3–0 in the ninth inning. They scored three runs. They loaded the bases. Steve Finley hit a **walk-off** grand slam!

TOUGH DAYS

The toughest day for the Dodgers was in 1951. The Giants beat them in a **playoff** game. Bobby Thomson hit a ninth-inning home run. It sent the Giants to the World Series. Here are a few other days Dodgers fans would like to forget.

1941—The Dodgers needed a win to tie the World Series against the Yankees. They were one strike away. A Yankees batter swung and missed! But the ball got away from the catcher. The batter was safe at first base. The Yankees rallied for four runs. New York won the game. The next day, they won the series.

Yasiel Puig can't believe the Dodgers ➤
just lost Game 7 of the 2017 World Series.

1962—The Dodgers played another playoff with the Giants. The winner would go to the World Series. Los Angeles needed three outs. Then, the Giants rallied in the ninth. San Francisco won 6–4.

2017—The World Series came down to Game 7. The Dodgers were at home against Houston. Ace pitcher Yu Darvish was pitching for LA. But the Astros went ahead in the first inning. They won 5–1.

MEET THE FANS!

Los Angeles fans love their team. It is said they "bleed Dodger Blue"! In 1978, more than three million fans went to the team's home games. The Dodgers were the first big-league team to reach that mark. The fans haven't stopped going to Dodger Stadium ever since! The Dodgers are always among the league leaders in attendance.

◄ *The outfield seats at a ballpark are called "bleachers."*
Dodgers fans pack the bleachers on sunny days.

HEROES THEN

The Dodgers have been known for great pitchers. Sandy Koufax, Don Drysdale, and Don Sutton are in the Hall of Fame. The team has had some very good hitters, too. Duke Snider and Gil Hodges were big sluggers. The most famous Dodgers player was infielder Jackie Robinson. In 1947, he became modern baseball's first black player.

Snider was known as "The Duke of Flatbush." ➤
That was the neighborhood near Ebbets Field in Brooklyn.

23

HEROES NOW

Clayton Kershaw is another great Dodgers pitcher. He has won the award as the NL's best pitcher three times. The team has some really good batters, too. Justin Turner is a top-hitting infielder. First baseman Cody Bellinger started 2017 in the **minor leagues**. He joined the team in late April. Then he hit 39 homers! That broke the NL **rookie** record.

◀ *Clayton Kershaw led the NL in strikeouts three times.*

GEARING UP

aseball players wear team uniforms. On defense, they wear leather gloves to catch the ball. As batters, they wear hard helmets. This protects them from pitches. Batters hit the ball with long wood bats. Each player chooses his own size of bat. Catchers have the toughest job. They wear a lot of protection.

THE BASEBALL

The outside of the Major League baseball is made from cow leather. Two leather pieces shaped like 8s are stitched together. There are 108 stitches of red thread. These stitches help players grip the ball. Inside, the ball has a small center of cork and rubber. Hundreds of feet of yarn are tightly wound around this center.

CATCHER'S HELMET ➤

CHEST PROTECTOR ➤

WRIST BANDS ◄

PITCH CHART ◄

CATCHER'S MITT ◄

SHIN GUARDS ➤

CATCHER'S GEAR

TEAM STATS

Here are some of the all-time career records for the Los Angeles Dodgers. All of these stats are through the 2018 regular season.

HOME RUNS

Duke Snider	389
Gil Hodges	361

RBI

Duke Snider	1,271
Gil Hodges	1,254

BATTING AVERAGE

Willie Keeler	.352
Babe Herman	.339

STOLEN BASES

Maury Wills	490
Davey Lopes	418

WINS

Don Sutton	233
Don Drysdale	209

SAVES

Kenley Jansen	268
Eric Gagne	161

Don Sutton pitched for the Dodgers for 16 sesaons. ➤

STRIKEOUTS	
Don Sutton	2,696
Don Drysdale	2,486

GLOSSARY

dodge (DAHJ) to suddenly move out of the way of something

minor leagues (MY-ner LEEGZ) the levels of baseball below MLB

playoff (PLAY-off) a game or series played between top teams to determine who moves ahead

rivals (RYE-vuhls) two people or groups competing for the same thing

rookie (ROOK-ee) a player in his first year of pro sports

sign (SYN) add a player to a team by giving them a contract to play

walk-off (WAHK-off) in baseball, a play that immediately results in the winning run

World Series (WURLD SEER-eez) the championship of Major League Baseball, played between the winners of the AL and NL

FIND OUT MORE

IN THE LIBRARY

Connery-Boyd, Peg. *The Los Angeles Dodgers: Big Book of Activities*. Chicago: Sourcebooks Jabberwocky, 2016.

Kelly, David A. *The L.A. Dodger (Ballpark Mysteries)*. New York, NY: Random House Books for Young Readers, 2011.

Rhodes, Sam. *Los Angeles Dodgers (Inside MLB)*. Calgary, AB: Weigl Publishing, 2018.

ON THE WEB

Visit our website for links about the Los Angeles Dodgers:
childsworld.com/links

Note to Parents, Teachers, and Librarians: We routinely verify our web links to make sure they are safe and active sites. So encourage your readers to check them out!

INDEX